The Veil

Wanda Luthman

Lilacs in Literature

Copyright © 2022 by Wanda Luthman

All rights reserved. No part of this publication may be reproduced, distributed, or transmitted in any form or by any means, electronic or mechanical, including photocopying and recording, or stored in any information storage and retrieval system, without permission in writing from the publisher, except in the case of brief quotations embedded in a review or certain other noncommercial uses permitted by US copyright law. For permissions requests, please write to wandalu64@gmail.com with the subject line "Request for Permissions"

Written by Wanda Luthman

Book Cover design and interior illustrations by Mara Reitsma

Proofread by Traci Sanders

ISBN: 978-1-7340099-6-5

Publisher: Lilacs in Literature

Cocoa, FL 32926

Contact Name: Wanda Luthman

Website: www.wandaluthman.wordpress.com

Contents

1. The Veil   1

Chapter 1

The Veil

"Father, Father, please help me with the belt to my tunic," Samuel pleaded.

"Come here, my son. Are you ready to read the Torah for our family today, your thirteenth birthday?" his father asked.

"Yes, Father. I am prepared. Thank you for helping me with my belt."

The boy's birthday fell on a Thursday this year, the day before the Jewish Passover, which was to begin at sundown the following night. As was custom on a boy's thirteenth birthday, Samuel would read and pray before his family for the first time, signifying his manhood.

Father said, "We are from the tribe of Levi, the tribe that Yahweh (God) appointed to serve Him in His tabernacle. You have been reading and studying the Torah from a young age under Rabbi Menechachen, who has said he saw much promise in you from the beginning. You understand teachings and have always been hungry and eager to learn more. You are my first-born son. I pray you will be chosen this year to serve as the Priest's understudy in the Tabernacle. This is a big day. Make me proud."

"I will, Father. I have chosen my passage carefully and have practiced every day."

Samuel had chosen his favorite passage from the ancient prophet of Isaiah (Isaiah 53).

Samuel's mother had been busy cooking and cleaning to prepare their home for this special day. Everything was ready. All of Samuel's younger siblings were clean and dressed neatly. They sat on the floor in a line, waiting for Samuel. Then, Rabbi Menechachen and the Priest came to the front door. Samuel's father welcomed them inside, and they were given the best chairs in the home.

Father spoke first, "Welcome, everyone, to this special day for Samuel, our son, who is turning thirteen today. On this day, he becomes a man."

Rabbi Menechachen stood and said, "Samuel, my son, whom I have had the pleasure of training in the reading of the Torah. Today, you have been given the privilege of reading a passage from the Torah in front of your family, myself, and the Priest. What passage have you chosen?"

Samuel stood and said, "Rabbi Menechachen, I have enjoyed learning from you, and I thank you for the time you have spent teaching me. For this day, I have chosen my favorite passage from the ancient prophet, Isaiah. It speaks about a time when Yahweh will send someone who would be like a lamb slaughtered for the sins of Israel. It seemed appropriate to read this since my birthday is just before Passover, which is our celebration of Yahweh rescuing the Jews from the Egyptians. Each family had slaughtered a first-born male lamb without blemish and painted their doorway with its blood to protect them from the Angel of Death, so he would pass by their home."

"You have chosen well, Samuel. Please begin," Rabbi Menechachen said.

In Samuel's native Hebrew tongue, he read the following:

"Isaiah, Chapter Fifty-three. Who hath believed our report? and to whom is the arm of the Lord revealed?

For he shall grow up before him as a tender plant, and as a root out of a dry ground: he hath no form nor comeliness; and when we shall see him, there is no beauty that we should desire him He is despised and rejected of men; a man of sorrows, and acquainted with grief: and we hid as it were our faces from him; he was despised, and we esteemed him not. Surely he hath borne our griefs, and carried our sorrows: yet we did esteem him stricken, smitten of God, and afflicted. But he was wounded for our transgressions, he was bruised for our iniquities: the chastisement of our peace was upon him; and with his stripes we are healed. All we like sheep have gone astray; we have turned every one to his own way; and the Lord hath laid on him the iniquity of us all. He was oppressed, and he was afflicted, yet he opened not his mouth: he is brought as a lamb to the slaughter, and as a sheep before her shearers is dumb, so he openeth not his mouth. He was taken from prison and from

THE VEIL

judgment: and who shall declare his generation? for he was cut off out of the land of the living: for the transgression of my people was he stricken. And he made his grave with the wicked, and with the rich in his death; because he had done no violence, neither was any deceit in his mouth. Yet it pleased the Lord to bruise him; he hath put him to grief: when thou shalt make his soul an offering for sin, he shall see his seed, he shall prolong his days, and the pleasure of the Lord shall prosper in his hand. He shall see of the travail of his soul, and shall be satisfied: by his knowledge shall my righteous servant justify many; for he shall bear their iniquities. Therefore will I divide him a portion with the great, and he shall divide the spoil with the strong; because he hath poured out his soul unto death: and he was numbered with the transgressors; and he bare the sin of many, and made intercession for the transgressors."

Then, Samuel asked everyone to bow their heads as he prayed… "Most High Yahweh, we come before you in humility and thank you for all you have given us and provided for us this day and throughout the ages. You rescued us from our oppressors, the Egyptians, many years ago and gave us good province in the land of Canaan. We celebrate your mighty hand of deliverance and gifts of prosperity and provision. May glory and honor be upon our lips towards you forevermore."

Samuel's father and mother rose and went and stood before him. They placed a special mantel, that his mother had made him, around his shoulders. This mantel was made of fine woven cloth and had upon it the family symbol. This signified the end of the ceremony and the acceptance of Samuel as a man within his family and to the community.

After the bestowing of the family mantel, Rabbi Menechachen and the Priest approached him.

Rabbi Menechachen took his hand in both of his and bowed his head slightly saying, "My boy, my son, today you have become a man. The passage you read shows great wisdom and insight. You are well-studied and have made this old Rabbi very glad."

The Priest then stepped forward and said, "My young Samuel, I have made my final decision. I'm inviting you to participate in this year's Passover rites as my understudy. This is a high honor, and my decision was not made lightly. Do you accept my invitation?"

Samuel's eyes grew wide with excitement. "Yes! Yes! I do, Priest. I have longed and hoped and dreamed to be chosen. I'm so very grateful and humbled and honored that you have chosen me this year. I will do my absolute best."

"I know you will. Now, go pack your things. We must be going," the Priest replied.

As Samuel ran upstairs to pack, his parents each took the hand of the Priest and thanked him for this special honor bestowed upon their boy and their entire family.

Samuel quickly packed his satchel. When he returned, his parents were standing with Rabbi Menechachen and the Priest, smiling with pride.

His mother drew him into her arms and hugged him tightly. She spoke softly with a slight hitch in her throat, "Samuel, I'm so very proud of you for being chosen to serve in the Tabernacle. Be a good young man and serve Yahweh well."

She kissed both of his cheeks.

"I will, Mother," he replied.

Then, his father shook his hand firmly, looking into his eyes, and said, "You are a man today, my son. Serve us and the tribe of Levi well in the Tabernacle."

"I will, Father," Samuel replied.

He turned to leave and paused as the doorknob met his hand. The thought occurred to him that he would never return to his home again to live. He ran back and gave his father a hug. His father squeezed him quickly and patted his back gruffly and said, "Good-bye."

Samuel thought he saw a tear run down his father's cheek. He straightened his posture and offered a final forced, "Good-bye," and left.

Rabbi Menechachen and the Priest had already gone ahead, so he ran to catch up to them. When they reached the Priest's home, Rabbi Menechachen said, "I will bid you farewell here and see you again after Passover. You did well today."

"Thank you, Rabbi. I have you to thank for teaching me so well all these years. I will make you proud. I promise. Good-bye," Samuel said.

"Good-bye," the Rabbi said and then quickly disappeared into the crowd.

The Priest opened the door to his home and gestured for Samuel to follow him. He went upstairs and showed him the room that was to be his, and the special clothes he would wear for the ceremony.

Then he said, "Dinner is promptly at six. Come dressed in your tunic and belt as you are now. After dinner, you will return to your room and do your studies. Bedtime is precisely at eight o'clock. You will rise at six in the morning without my assistance and breakfast is at seven. Afterwards, you will accompany me to the temple."

He turned and left quickly, closing the door behind him.

Samuel sat on the cot and said to himself, "This day has been more wonderful than I could have even imagined."

A quiet sense of awe washed over him as tears filled his eyes, "I knew Yahweh was doing something special in my life."

At precisely six, he arrived downstairs. The Priest sat without a word and then motioned for the boy to sit across from him. Samuel pulled out the wooden chair and sat.

The Priest folded his hands and closed his eyes, so Samuel did the same. The Priest prayed, "O Most Holy and Mighty Yahweh, thank you for this meal. May we never forget that you are our provider."

The Priest served the vegetable soup and dry bread to Samuel. Then he served himself. The two sat in silence as they ate.

Afterwards, the Priest said, "Pick up your dishes and follow me."

They went outside to a small water basin where they each washed and dried their own dishes, then returned inside and placed them on the counter for the next use.

The Priest said, "Samuel, return to your room and study the scroll that I have chosen for you."

Samuel nodded and climbed the narrow staircase to his room. There, he knelt by his cot and prayed, "Most Holy, High Yahweh, thank you for the opportunity to serve you and your people. Please grant me the wisdom to understand my studies and help me to be a worthy servant."

Then, he opened the scroll the Priest had selected for him. He carefully unrolled it.

He gasped, "Now I know Yahweh has selected me this day to serve Him because this is the very prophet I read from today at my thirteenth birthday celebration. Neither Rabbi Menechachen nor the Priest knew I was going to read from the prophet Isaiah."

That silent awe he felt earlier surrounded him again. He read until eight that evening. Then, he blew out the candle on the table next to his cot and fell fast asleep.

He woke with the first ray of sun and dressed quickly, then went downstairs.

The Priest was waiting for him with a stern look in his eyes. Samuel bowed his head and said, "I apologize, Priest, if I was late."

The Priest sat and motioned for him to sit as well. Again, they ate in silence and washed and dried their dishes.

The Priest said, "Return to your room and dress yourself in the woven tunic and leather belt I have provided for you for this day. Be sure to latch your sandals and wear your mantel that your parents bestowed upon you yesterday. Wait for me. I will call you when we are ready to leave."

Samuel did as he was told. He followed the Priest's instructions exactly and sat on his cot to wait.

He bowed his head, "O Most High, Holy Yahweh, allow me to be pleasing to the Priest. I do not want to disappoint him or you. I want to make my family and the community proud."

After a long while, the Priest called for him, and he descended the stairs.

The Priest said, "Come, let us go now."

They left and walked through the crowded streets to the Tabernacle. There were people from many cities and towns far and near, and livestock in the streets of Jerusalem. They had all come for Passover.

They walked through the crowds and overheard people discussing the activities that had occurred overnight. Apparently, a man named Yeshuah (Jesus, which means *God is salvation* or *God is deliverance, protection, rescue, freedom, refuge, and safety*) had been found guilty of the highest heresy—calling himself equal to God. He had been condemned to die on a cross just outside the city. Samuel had heard rumors of this man who went around healing people. He was puzzled that such a kind man would think himself equal to Yahweh and not realize his error once he was brought before a Court of Law.

Then, Samuel and the Priest entered the Outer Gate of the Tabernacle. It was just at the time of a staff change. They watched as families with children,

THE VEIL

couples, and single people all brought their first-born choice livestock to be sacrificed for their sins.

Samuel said, "I have come many times with my family with our chosen lamb and understand the importance and significance and contrition of heart in this holy activity."

The Priest nodded at him but didn't say a word.

As Samuel was contemplating this, he and the Priest watched the other priests perform their duties, and then the Priest said, "Come, let us wash our hands in the basin."

As they were drying their hands, another priest brought sacrificial blood in a bowl to them and, taking a hyssop branch, dipped it into the blood. He recited an ancient prayer in Hebrew and flicked the blood over their heads and upon their garments.

The Priest said, "This concludes the cleansing ritual that must be performed before we enter the Holy Place."

Samuel's heart pounded with excitement, and he said, "I am humbled and honored to be partaking in this most holy ritual that few have had the privilege to experience. I feel a spiritual connection to all the priests who have ever served."

"Indeed, participating in ancient rituals does connect us with our past," the Priest replied.

The Priest led Samuel to another area. There were twelve loaves of showbread carefully arranged in a basket, and a bowl of olive oil.

He said, "Tomorrow morning, we will wake before sunrise and come to the Tabernacle and cleanse ourselves in order to take these items into the Holy Place at the prescribed time. You will take the basket of showbread and remove the loaves that are lying on the table and replace them with the fresh showbread. I will check the oil in the lampstands. You are not to talk or ask me any questions while we are inside. Do you understand?"

"Yes," Samuel replied.

"Do you have any questions before I take you inside to show you?"

"No, sir."

They went to the entrance of the Holy Place, bowed their heads, and offered a simple prayer, "O Most Holy Yahweh, please accept the cleansing of our bodies through the ancient rituals you have given our forefathers that we may enter the Holy Place in peace and safety."

After they walked inside the Holy Place and closed the door behind them, a sacred hush filled the place. All the outside noise and chatter stopped. The Priest led Samuel to the table with the showbread, and Samuel nodded with understanding. There lay the loaves he would remove in the morning and replace with the fresh loaves. They were lined up in rows of three. Samuel observed exactly how they were placed so he would know what to do. Then, the Priest led him to the lampstands and pointed to the opening where he would refill them with the olive oil. Samuel nodded as he watched how it was done. Then, the Priest led him to the incense that continually burned before the curtain to the Holiest of Holies, the most sacred place where Yahweh himself lived. Only the High Priest could enter this place, and only after being thoroughly cleansed. Otherwise, they would die.

Samuel reminded himself of the ancient writings of Moses when Yahweh had given him instructions on how to build the Tabernacle. All the Jewish people offered their gold and bronze and precious stones to be used in the making of the things inside. It was indeed beautiful.

Yahweh had given precise instructions on how long and wide the Tabernacle should be and exactly how the lampstands should be created, having three branches and three lamps on each branch. This was all just as he'd imagined, only even more beautiful. There was a glow to the room that seemed to come from a source greater than the light of the lampstands.

Just then, they heard a loud rumble and the ground beneath them began to shake. The showbread that moments before had been neatly lined up on the table, now had fallen onto the floor. The Priest grabbed the lampstand to prevent it from toppling over.

Then, to their left, they heard a loud ripping sound. They both looked at the curtain separating the Holy Place from the Holiest of Holies where only the High Priest could go in, and only once a year on a prescribed date. Today was not that day.

THE VEIL

Fear gripped their hearts. This was no ordinary curtain. It was made from seven layers of thick animal skins and two layers of finely woven fabric. This curtain was indestructible. But, furthermore, what existed beyond the curtain was the Holiest of Holies, which housed the mercy seat of Yahweh.

Inside the mercy seat were the Ten Commandments that Yahweh had written himself and given to Moses for the Jewish people on Mount Sinai. It also housed Aaron's rod that sprouted. There were two exceptionally large golden cherubim overlooking the mercy seat. Also, in the Holiest of Holies there was another lampstand.

Samuel and the Priest knew from their studies that if the curtain ripped and they were exposed to the mercy seat, they would die.

Just then, the curtain ripped all the way down from top to bottom as the rumbling sound continued and the ground trembled.

Suddenly, a bright light shone forth from the opening. The Priest threw himself to the ground, grabbing the boy to bow down also and then shielded Samuel with his body - a beautiful, sacrificial gesture to try and spare the young man.

Then, the rumbling stopped, and both turned to see if the rip supernaturally repaired itself or if it had just been a miracle because neither of them should have been alive, otherwise.

But, to their surprise and terror, the rip had indeed occurred, and the curtain was in two pieces. A beautiful, warm light shone from within and somehow it was as though they could "feel" the light. It enveloped them and seeped into their lungs when they breathed.

Samuel knew he wasn't supposed to speak but couldn't help himself, "I feel like something that I have been missing and searching for my whole life, longing for even, has found me. I feel a profound peace."

The Priest nodded.

A voice, the voice of Yahweh said, "Do not be afraid for, today, you have been redeemed."

The Priest stretched out his hands on the ground and laid prostrate, keeping his face to the ground in a position of humility and praise. Samuel did the same.

The Priest said, "Yahweh, we are not worthy of your presence or grace. Thank you for sparing our lives."

Samuel nodded in agreement. Tears rolled down both of their faces.

Then, a loud voice, the voice of Yeshua, said, "It is finished, Father."

Another voice, Yahweh's, spoke. "Your sacrifice has been accepted. Go now, empowered with the Holy Spirit, and complete your missions."

A dove fluttered from beyond the curtain and then flew past them and outside. The curtain opened as if a person were pulling it back and walking through it.

Samuel and the Priest both felt a presence pass by as the curtain fell back in place. The glowing light then also pierced through the entrance to the outside. The people outside were rising to their feet and brushing off their clothes. Children were crying and clinging to their parents. The livestock were shuffling against their leads. And just as suddenly as the light had filled the room, it was gone.

Samuel and the Priest still felt the warmth but knew the moment was over. The Priest said, "Samuel, the showbread, it's gone."

Samuel looked at what had fallen on the ground. The showbread was no longer there, and it wasn't on top of the table either. The Priest then went to look in the lampstands. They were no longer filled with oil and the light had gone out in each. Yet, none had spilled or leaked out.

They looked at one another in bewilderment. The Priest said, "Something strange has indeed happened here today."

Samuel replied, "Indeed. I cannot explain it."

They left quietly and headed back to the Priest's home. Along the way, they heard chatter about the crucifixion and how when the man that claimed to be Yahweh died, he had uttered the words, "It is finished."

A chill ran up Samuel's back. People had said at the very moment the man died is when the earthquake happened. The Priest looked at Samuel and nodded. They quickened their pace to the Priest's home. Once inside, the Priest closed the door behind them and locked it. He pulled the shutters tight on his windows. He lit the logs in the fireplace and began warming the soup and spiced wine.

Then, he spoke in a whisper, "I think the man they crucified today was the Messiah, the Christ, the long-awaited one."

Samuel agreed and ran upstairs to get the scroll from the prophet Isaiah. He began reading from it, and every prophecy had been fulfilled.

They stared into each other's eyes knowing they had experienced something no one else had. Something that had brought clarity to the prophet Isaiah's words.

"Tomorrow, you must go and tell one of his disciples what we witnessed. They need to know that their teacher, Yeshua, was truly The One they had been waiting for; the Messiah," the Priest commanded Samuel.

They spoke late into the evening until Samuel finally went upstairs to his cot. He lay there contemplating the past two days and how Yahweh had indeed called him to the service of the Tabernacle.

In the morning, he woke up early, dressed, and went downstairs for breakfast. The Priest and he didn't speak much—only to pray and confirm Samuel's task for the day.

Samuel left to go search for one of Yeshua's disciples, but everyone he asked did not seem to know where he could find any of them. Finally, someone told him they could take him to Mary's (Yeshua's mother's) house. When they arrived at her humble home, she welcomed them in, but the companion said they could not stay.

She held the door open for Samuel and stood aside and beckoned him inside with her hand. She told him to take a seat at the wooden table. He sat down, and she sat across from him and looked into his eyes. Finally, she spoke, "What brings you to see me?"

Samuel told her all that he and the Priest had experienced the day before.

She listened intently. Then, a smile formed on her lips.

She replied, "The man who died on the cross yesterday was the prophesied Messiah. I was told of it before he was born. He fulfilled all the prophecies about himself. He lived an innocent life and loved others and performed many miracles. He died for us. He told us this beforehand so we would understand. He was the sacrificial lamb who came to die once and for all. Animal sacrifices are no longer necessary. He has opened the curtain for us to have a direct relationship with Yahweh, the Most High Yahweh/His Father, just like Adam and Eve did in the Garden of Eden. Just as it was originally intended before sin entered the world. Do you believe this?"

Samuel replied, "Yes, I believe all you have said."

"Then you are saved from the wrath of Yahweh. You will live forever in Yahweh's Kingdom. Now, go and tell others the good news. For all who believe shall be saved," she said.

"I will. Yes, ma'am, I will. I am so thankful I came to see you and told you about what happened in the Tabernacle, for you confirmed that Yeshua, the one who died yesterday on the cross, was indeed our Messiah," Samuel replied.

"Indeed. It is good you came, but even better that you believe," she said.

She stood and went around the table. She pulled him into her arms and hugged him warmly.

Samuel felt a stirring in his soul, and he suddenly knew where to begin telling the marvelous story of The Veil.

If you would like to know the real and living Yeshua, Jesus, described in this book, you can. All you need to do is pray the following prayer:

In Romans Chapter 10, verses 9 and 10 it says, "...that if you confess with your mouth the Lord Jesus

and believe in your heart that God has raised Him from the dead, you will be saved. For with the heart one believes unto righteousness, and with the mouth, confession is made unto salvation."

THE VEIL

Pray this prayer, "Dear Jesus, I believe you are the Son of God who died and rose again on the third

day to forgive us of our sins. I ask you, today, to please forgive me of my sins and come into my heart to live that I might have salvation and eternal life in you. Amen"

Now, you are saved. Go and spread His love in all the worldIf you prayed this prayer, I would love to hear from you.

Please reach out to me at wandalu64@gmail.com and put in the Subject Line: "The Veil, I prayed the prayer"

Also, if you would like a FREE 30-Day Devotional written by

me, you can download it for FREE at http://eepurl.com/bZT579

Other biblical fiction books by Wanda Luthman are The Cloak.

Available on Amazon in paperback, ebook, and audiobook. Visit myBook.to/Cloak

Wanda Luthman's Biography

Wanda Luthman is an international multi-award-winning author. She's been a Christian since she was 3 years old, was baptized at 12 years old, and attended a Christian College in the Midwest double majoring in Psychology and Sociology. She has practiced in the field of counseling for over 20 years. But, she felt she really "met" God in her late 40's when her Pastor taught her contemplative listening which is a Christian form of meditation. Since then, she's been on a mission to share God's love with everyone she meets.

www.ingramcontent.com/pod-product-compliance
Lightning Source LLC
Chambersburg PA
CBHW072138070526
44585CB00016B/1737